First published in 2017 by Emma Davies

Copyright Emma Davies 2017

"A Year With My Camera" is a registered trademark.

ISBN: 978-0-9956324-2-4

EmmaDaviesPhotography.com

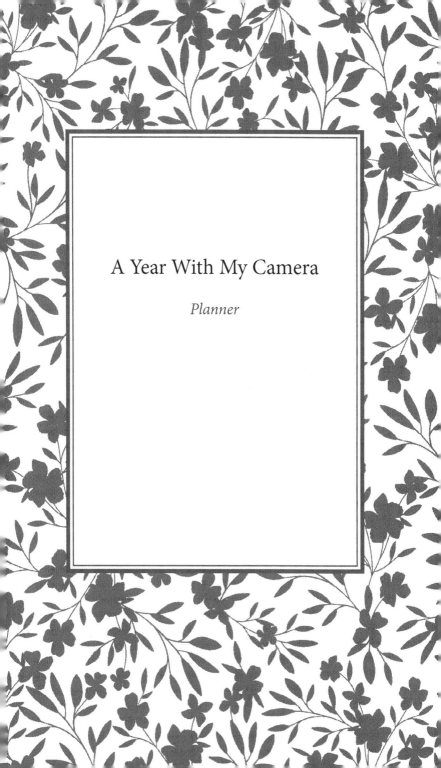

A Year With My Camera

Planner

About A Year With My Camera

A Year With My Camera is a beginner's photography course, carefully structured to get you off auto and keep you off auto. You can't learn photography in a weekend, so rather than waste what precious spare time you have trying to pick up bits and pieces of knowledge here and there, A Year With My Camera is designed to take you steadily through everything you need to know. You learn one thing a week. By the end of 6 weeks you will be off auto. By the end of 3 months you'll be taking photos you're proud of. And by the end of the year you'll be the best photographer you know.

How to use this planner

I designed this planner at the request of students who wanted the weekly projects and reminders in one place, small enough to carry around. This version is undated, so it doesn't matter what time of year you start the course. The planner doesn't have the actual lessons - just the reminders. You'll still need to either have the workbooks (available on Amazon), the video course (see website: AYearWithMyCamera.com) or have signed up for the emails at AYearWithMyCamera.com.

When you first join the course, open up the planner at Week 1. Write in your starting date, and then as you progress through the course, fill in the subsequent dates so you can see what you should be doing and when.

The planner follows the order of the workbooks, the video course and the emails, except for the Travel module. The Travel module is not included in the free emails (we do 30 Days of Composition instead). If you don't have Workbook 2 or the video lessons, do 30 Days of Composition along with everyone else doing the free email course, and ignore the Travel prompts in this planner. 30 Days of Composition was originally conceived as a summer break activity and if you start your course on 1 January, then it coincides broadly speaking with August in this planner. If you start your course later in the year you can either do 30 Days of Composition when it arrives, or take a break and do it in August anyway.

If you want to do #1Day12Pics each month, mark them in now, on the 1st Saturday of every month.

#Make30Photos

#Make30Photos is a 30 day photo challenge with a twist: you don't have to finish it in 30 days. Take as long as you like; the only requirement is to think about your photo before you take it – make it, don't take it. The challenge does not form part of A Year With My Camera, but many students like the challenge and have asked for all the prompts in one place.

If you're on Instagram, use the #Make30Photos hashtag.

- [ ] fill the frame with colour
- [ ] things in threes
- [ ] black and white
- [ ] taken at midday
- [ ] abstract
- [ ] snail's eye view
- [ ] reflection
- [ ] lit by a window
- [ ] older than me
- [ ] food
- [ ] shadows
- [ ] plain background
- [ ] balance
- [ ] urban
- [ ] extreme edit
- [ ] eyecatching
- [ ] behind the scenes
- [ ] pattern
- [ ] wildlife
- [ ] break the rule of thirds
- [ ] just two colours
- [ ] move the camera
- [ ] self portrait
- [ ] movement
- [ ] stripes
- [ ] weather
- [ ] silhouette
- [ ] depth
- [ ] vintage
- [ ] texture

#30DaysOfComposition

#30DaysOfComposition traditionally forms the summer break on the A Year With My Camera course. It's a chance to reinforce your composition skills, and learn some new techniques. If you start the course in January, this challenge falls in August. If you start the course any other time of year, either fit the prompts in around the other modules, or take a break when you feel like it. You will find the prompts in weeks 33-36 in this planner.

If you're on Instagram, use the #30DaysOfComposition hashtag.

- [ ] viewpoint
- [ ] framing
- [ ] negative space
- [ ] diagonals
- [ ] rule of thirds
- [ ] leading lines
- [ ] symmetry
- [ ] fill the frame
- [ ] threes or fives
- [ ] balance
- [ ] pattern
- [ ] no foreground
- [ ] circular
- [ ] form or shape
- [ ] texture

- [ ] what's leaving the frame?
- [ ] create depth
- [ ] create movement
- [ ] perfectly aligned
- [ ] deliberately discordant
- [ ] square format
- [ ] single focal point
- [ ] tiny subject
- [ ] complementary colour
- [ ] mono
- [ ] abstract
- [ ] repetition
- [ ] S-curve
- [ ] eye contact
- [ ] break the rules

WEEK 1: Exposure

INTRODUCTION TO EXPOSURE: Book 1 Ch 1

How does the camera decide how much light to let in?

Why is 18% grey important?

What happens when you take a photo of white paper, on any auto mode?

What happens when you take a photo of black paper, on any auto mode?

NOTES

If you need to buy the workbooks, search for "A Year With My Camera" on your local Amazon store.

Use the #AYearWithMyCamera hashtag on Instagram.

Date:

HOMEWORK

- [ ] white paper
- [ ] black paper

TO DO

Mark in all the
#1Day12Pics dates - the
first Saturday of every
month.

TO THINK ABOUT

There are 3 quotes that
sum up the A Year With
My Camera way of doing
things. Which one appeals
to you most?

"The only photographer I
will compare myself to is
the one I used to be."

"Never, ever
underestimate the
importance of having fun."

"Progress, not perfection."

Monday	
Tuesday	
Wednesday	
Thursday	
Friday	
Saturday	
Sunday	

WEEK 2: Aperture

DEPTH OF FIELD: Book 1 Ch 2

Size of aperture controls depth of field in image.

Large hole = small depth of field.

Small hole = large depth of field.

f4 = large hole, f16 = small hole.

Remember to focus on your subject.

NOTES

Date:

HOMEWORK

Use aperture priority mode.

☐ largest aperture
☐ smallest aperture

less depth of field

↑

f2.8

f4

f5.6

f8

f11

f16

f22

more depth of field

Monday	
Tuesday	
Wednesday	
Thursday	
Friday	
Saturday	
Sunday	

WEEK 3: Shutter speed

PLAYING WITH TIME: Book 1 Ch 3

Shutter speed controls the sharpness (or blur) of anything moving in your image.

Too slow a shutter speed will also result in camera shake if you are not using a tripod.

NOTES

Date:

HOMEWORK

Use shutter priority mode.

☐ slow shutter speed
☐ fast shutter speed

Fireworks, light painting	10 sec
Blur moving water	1/8
Minimum for handheld	1/60
A good starting point	1/125
Children playing	1/250
Sports, flowers in a breeze	1/500
Freeze water splashes, moving cars	1/1000

Monday

Tuesday

Wednesday

Thursday

Friday

Saturday

Sunday

WEEK 4: ISO

SENSOR SENSITIVITY: Book 1 Ch 4

High ISO = very sensitive sensor = use in dark conditions.
Low ISO = less sensitive sensor = use in bright conditions.

High ISO = more noise or grain in final image.
Low ISO = less noise; better quality final image.

NOTES

Date:

HOMEWORK

☐ Auto ISO?

☐ Redo aperture/shutter speed homework, with ISO as a backup

less sensitive
less noise

50

100

200

400

800

1600

3200

more sensitive
more noise

Monday
Tuesday
Wednesday
Thursday
Friday
Saturday
Sunday

WEEK 5: Exposure triangle

STOPS: Book 1 Ch 5

1 stop of light = the amount between full increments of aperture, shutter speed and ISO.

1 full stop aperture = 1 full stop shutter speed = 1 full stop ISO.

NOTES

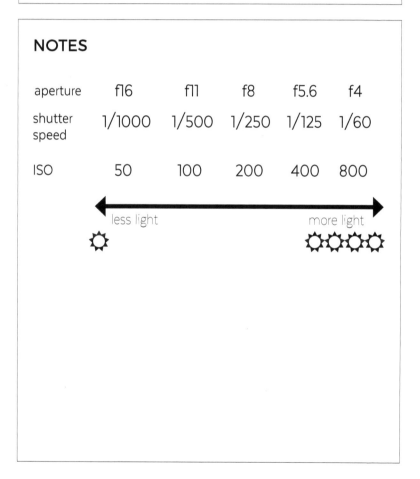

aperture	f16	f11	f8	f5.6	f4
shutter speed	1/1000	1/500	1/250	1/125	1/60
ISO	50	100	200	400	800

Date:

HOMEWORK

Use aperture priority mode.

☐ Change the camera's settings by 1 stop of aperture, and compensate with 1 stop of shutter speed.

TO DO

Try Instagram. Use the #AYearWithMyCamera hashtag.

Monday	
Tuesday	
Wednesday	
Thursday	
Friday	
Saturday	
Sunday	

WEEK 6: Metering

GETTING THE EXPOSURE CORRECT: Book 1 Ch 6

Which metering mode are you using?

Do you understand what the histogram is telling you?

Can you use the histogram to check the exposure?

Don't forget the histogram never lies.

The exposure compensation dial is very useful for quick fixes.

NOTES

Date:

HOMEWORK

- [ ] spend a day with the histogram switched on

- [ ] check histogram when taking a photo of a piece of white paper

- [ ] try using exposure compensation to correct metering errors

Monday

Tuesday

Wednesday

Thursday

Friday

Saturday

Sunday

WEEK 7: Have a break

Notes from the Exposure module

Exposure module review: what do you know now that you didn't, 6 weeks ago?

Date:

	Monday
	Tuesday
	Wednesday
	Thursday
	Friday
	Saturday
	Sunday

END OF EXPOSURE MODULE - TEST

- [ ] shot with max aperture (biggest hole, smallest number)
- [ ] shot with min aperture (smallest hole, biggest number)
- [ ] shot at f8
- [ ] shutter speed of 1 second
- [ ] shutter speed of 1/1000th second
- [ ] shot with largest ISO
- [ ] small depth of field
- [ ] large depth of field
- [ ] creative camera shake
- [ ] subject in focus, background blurred
- [ ] background in focus, subject blurred
- [ ] everything in focus
- [ ] moving subject frozen & moving subject blurred
- [ ] shot at min focus distance and max aperture
- [ ] shot at min focus distance and min aperture

END OF EXPOSURE MODULE - PROJECTS

1. Depth of field study

2. White on white study

Have you joined the Facebook group?

AYearWithMyCamera.com/join-facebook

The only photographer I will compare myself to is the one I used to be.

WEEK 8: Composition 1

SUBJECT, BACKGROUND, FOREGROUND: Book 1 Ch 7

SUBJECT: one single clear subject

BACKGROUND: context and contrast, no distractions

FOREGROUND: introduces the subject, not overwhelming

Use viewpoint to change balance between each element.

NOTES

Date:

HOMEWORK

- ☐ mostly subject
- ☐ mostly foreground
- ☐ mostly background
- ☐ no subject
- ☐ no foreground
- ☐ no background
- ☐ pleasing balance

REVISION

- ☐ subject in focus, background blurred

TO THINK ABOUT

You are in control of where everything appears in the frame. Keep moving, and keep an eye on how each element interacts with all the other elements as you move.

Monday

Tuesday

Wednesday

Thursday

Friday

Saturday

Sunday

WEEK 9: Composition 2

SINGLE FOCAL POINT: Book 1 Ch 8

Eliminate unnecessary and distracting elements from the photograph. Use composition to draw attention to your single focal point:

1. size in relation to other elements
2. position in the frame
3. contrast with the background
4. separation from other elements
5. point to the subject (framing, leading lines)

NOTES

Date:

HOMEWORK

- [ ] just 1 subject
- [ ] relative size
- [ ] rule of thirds
- [ ] colour contrast
- [ ] blur the background
- [ ] no overlap
- [ ] framing
- [ ] leading lines

REVISION

- [ ] large depth of field

Monday	
Tuesday	
Wednesday	
Thursday	
Friday	
Saturday	
Sunday	

WEEK 10: Composition 3

DESIGN PRINCIPLES: Book 1 Ch 9

Use design principles for aesthetically pleasing images, and be deliberate about what you include in the frame. Check for distractions and keep moving.

NOTES

Date:

HOMEWORK

- ☐ 3s or 5s
- ☐ fill the frame
- ☐ symmetry
- ☐ natural diagonals
- ☐ dynamic repetition
- ☐ strong negative space

REVISION

- ☐ shot at your closest focussing distance

Monday	
Tuesday	
Wednesday	
Thursday	
Friday	
Saturday	
Sunday	

WEEK 11: Composition 4

ADVANCED COMPOSITION: Book 1 Ch 10

Why are you taking photographs?

What advanced techniques can you use to communicate with your viewer?

1. visual weight
2. what's out of frame?
3. what's leaving the frame?
4. what's overlapping?

NOTES

Date:

HOMEWORK

Communicate with your
viewer. Pick one:

melancholy
balanced
tired
expectant
happy
impatient
isolation
sinister
abundant
silent
timeless
persistent
distorted
true
impossible
old
complete

REVISION

☐   moving subject frozen

Monday	
Tuesday	
Wednesday	
Thursday	
Friday	
Saturday	
Sunday	

WEEK 12: Have a break

Notes from the Composition module

What have you enjoyed most so far? What can you do now
that you couldn't at the start? What do you want to work on?

Date:

	Monday
	Tuesday
	Wednesday
	Thursday
	Friday
	Saturday
	Sunday

END OF COMPOSITION MODULE - TEST

- [ ] mostly foreground
- [ ] no background at all
- [ ] 1 subject, 12 viewpoints
- [ ] make the sky the subject
- [ ] background separation
- [ ] rule of thirds
- [ ] single focal point
- [ ] a static image
- [ ] a dynamic image
- [ ] an image that leaves questions unanswered
- [ ] give too much visual weight to the background
- [ ] echo something from the subject in the background
- [ ] try and recreate a famous painting with your camera
- [ ] subject, background, foreground each 1/3 frame
- [ ] tell a story in 1 image

END OF COMPOSITION MODULE - PROJECT

Turning vision into reality

- [ ] safe
- [ ] Once upon a time...
- [ ] confused
- [ ] set in stone
- [ ] step by step

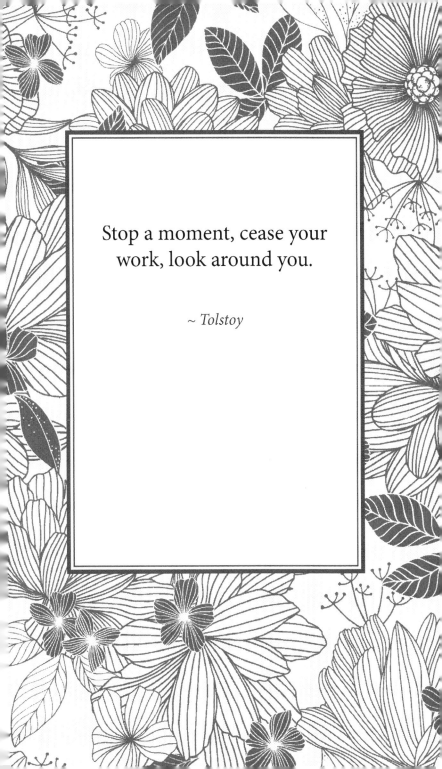

Stop a moment, cease your work, look around you.

~ Tolstoy

WEEK 13: Light 1

DIRECTION OF LIGHT: Book 1 Ch 11

Light is an element to any photograph all to itself.

The direction the light is coming from will influence the feel of your photograph.

You can control the direction of the light by either moving the light, or moving yourself.

NOTES

Date:

HOMEWORK

Light your subject:

- ☐ from above
- ☐ from below
- ☐ from the front
- ☐ from the back
- ☐ from the left
- ☐ from the right
- ☐ indoors/outdoors

REVISION

- ☐ 1 second exposure

Monday	
Tuesday	
Wednesday	
Thursday	
Friday	
Saturday	
Sunday	

WEEK 14: Light 2

NOTES

Date:

HOMEWORK

Go on a shadow safari.
Include:

- [ ] indirect window light
- [ ] outdoor shade
- [ ] overhead sunlight
- [ ] on-camera flash
- [ ] desklamp
- [ ] direct sun + diffuser
- [ ] cloudy day
- [ ] morning/evening

REVISION

- [ ] use the histogram to get the correct exposure when you take a photo of a piece of white paper

Monday	
Tuesday	
Wednesday	
Thursday	
Friday	
Saturday	
Sunday	

WEEK 15: Light 3

COLOUR OF LIGHT: Book 1 Ch 13

All light sources have a temperature which translates to a colour cast. On auto, your camera does its best to correct colour casts to a neutral white balance.

Colour temperature mistakes can be corrected beforehand by using manual white balance, or afterwards by using editing software.

NOTES

Date:

HOMEWORK

- ☐ work out how to change the white balance on your camera

- ☐ on Auto WB take a photo of something white in at least 3 different lighting conditions

- ☐ take the same 3 photos but on the Tungsten setting

- ☐ take the same 3 photos but on a manual Kelvin setting, eg, 7500K

REVISION

- ☐ take a photo on auto mode, write down the settings; change the aperture and the shutter speed but keep the exposure the same

---

Monday

Tuesday

Wednesday

Thursday

Friday

Saturday

Sunday

WEEK 16: Light 4

USING 2 LIGHTS: Book 1 Ch 14

Very strong, direct light gives high contrast images. To reduce contrast on your subject, use a fill light or a reflector.

NOTES

Date:

HOMEWORK

Using a strong, direct main light and a table-top subject, take 2 images:

- [ ] no reflector
- [ ] reflector

REVISION

- [ ] blur the background when you are at least 2 metres away from your subject

Monday

Tuesday

Wednesday

Thursday

Friday

Saturday

Sunday

WEEK 17: Have a break

Notes from the Light module

Have you started to see the light as an element all to itself in your images?

Date:

	Monday
	Tuesday
	Wednesday
	Thursday
	Friday
	Saturday
	Sunday

END OF LIGHT MODULE - CONSOLIDATE

- [ ] same subject lit 6 different ways
- [ ] contrejour (light behind the subject)
- [ ] hard shadows
- [ ] soft shadows
- [ ] no shadows
- [ ] use a diffuser
- [ ] use the wrong colour temperature setting
- [ ] 2 colours of light in the same photo
- [ ] shoot something white in 4 different colour temperatures, and make sure the white stays white in all 4
- [ ] find an HDR image and use the histogram to first expose for the highlights and then the shadows
- [ ] use a mirror as a reflector
- [ ] use a torch or phone screen light as a fill light
- [ ] use on-camera flash as a fill light for a back-lit subject
- [ ] make the light (or the shadows) the subject

END OF LIGHT MODULE - PROJECT

Take an image you are proud of.

- [ ] pick a motivating subject
- [ ] what do you want to say?
- [ ] which is the most important camera setting?
- [ ] build your composition carefully
- [ ] create the light, don't just let it happen

Done is better than perfect

WEEK 18: Creative 1

SETTING BOUNDARIES: Book 1 Ch 15

Set limits to release creativity; artificial ones if you need to.

Accept mistakes and less creative photos as necessary steps on your photographic journey.

Work on Auto mode for this module if you want to.

NOTES

Date:

HOMEWORK

- ☐ every 5 mins for an hour
- ☐ every 15 steps
- ☐ do a #1Day12Pics
- ☐ 10 mins: 20 photos
- ☐ 20 photos from 1 spot
- ☐ 20 photos of 1 thing
- ☐ toddler's viewpoint
- ☐ 20 shots of white paper
- ☐ 50 with 50
- ☐ 20 shots: small aperture
- ☐ 20 shots: least used kit
- ☐ 20 shots: 1 sec shutter

REVISION

- ☐ shot on your smallest aperture

Monday	
Tuesday	
Wednesday	
Thursday	
Friday	
Saturday	
Sunday	

WEEK 19: Creative 2

SELECTIVE ATTENTION: Book 1 Ch 16

Train yourself not just to look at a scene but to see all the details that will be needed to find and take your image.

Be aware of being distracted at the stage of looking for images, and also at the point when you are framing your image.

NOTES

Date:

HOMEWORK

- [ ] leave your camera at home
- [ ] just start
- [ ] 24 shots
- [ ] recreate another image
- [ ] frame with your hands

REVISION

- [ ] blur a moving subject

Monday
Tuesday
Wednesday
Thursday
Friday
Saturday
Sunday

WEEK 20: Creative 3

NOTHING IS ORIGINAL: Book 1 Ch 17

Use your energy to create photographs which are unique to you, rather than striving to be completely original.

Don't forget that no one else brings to the moment everything you have done, seen, read and experienced.

NOTES

Date:

HOMEWORK

Bring something of
yourself to your images.
How do your choices
affect your final image?

- [ ] viewpoint
- [ ] composition
- [ ] aperture
- [ ] lens choice

TO DO

Ask someone who knows
you well to give you 3 words
that describe you.

1:

2:

3:

REVISION

- [ ] 1/4000th shutter speed
  (or whatever your fastest
  is)

Monday

Tuesday

Wednesday

Thursday

Friday

Saturday

Sunday

WEEK 21: Creative 4

FINDING INSPIRATION: Book 1 Ch 18

3 stages to finding inspiration:

1. 20 minutes of brainstorming
2. 20 minutes of editing
3. incubation stage if needed

NOTES

Date:

HOMEWORK

- [ ] use the 3 step process to come up with an idea that is new to you

REVISION

- [ ] 3 second exposure

Monday	
Tuesday	
Wednesday	
Thursday	
Friday	
Saturday	
Sunday	

WEEK 22: Have a break

Notes from Creative module

Did you enjoy this module or do you prefer the more practical lessons?

Date:

	Monday
	Tuesday
	Wednesday
	Thursday
	Friday
	Saturday
	Sunday

END OF CREATIVE MODULE - CONSOLIDATE

- [ ] shoot at the same time every day for a month
- [ ] shoot the same thing in the same place every hour all day
- [ ] take 10 eye catching images using only your phone
- [ ] look up, and take a compelling image without moving
- [ ] shoot the same subject from a bird's and a snail's eye view
- [ ] make a fascinating photo shot from your head height
- [ ] compose an image, but shoot with your eyes closed
- [ ] focus your attention on just the background all day
- [ ] take 10 photos where you took 10 deep breaths before you pressed the shutter
- [ ] indulge yourself for a week - only take photos of things you love, on settings you are comfortable with, in a style that comes easily
- [ ] next time you are driving, walking or showering, think about what you would like to photograph next

END OF CREATIVE MODULE - PROJECT

Make something meaningful. Start with a person, a poem, a place or a painting that means something to you. Create a photograph that captures an element of what it means to you, however small.

Use the creativity exercises from this module to percolate a few ideas. Don't forget everything you've learnt about settings, composition and light. Print your photo and get it on the wall.

If you hear a voice within you say, "You cannot paint," then by all means paint, and that voice will be silenced.

~ *Vincent van Gogh*

WEEK 23: Edit 1

BASIC EDITS: Book 2 Ch 1

Editing is not cheating - photographers have always edited their images.

The 3 basic edits to consider for each photograph are: fixing exposure errors, fixing white balance errors, and cropping.

NOTES

Date:

HOMEWORK

- ☐ brighten an underexposed image
- ☐ darken an overexposed image
- ☐ fix the white balance on a yellow image
- ☐ fix the white balance on a blue image
- ☐ crop for a stronger composition
- ☐ crop to a square

TO DO

What are the pixel dimensions of your images straight out of camera? How much can you afford to crop?

REVISION

- ☐ use composition to create a dynamic image

Monday

Tuesday

Wednesday

Thursday

Friday

Saturday

Sunday

WEEK 24: Edit 2

COLOUR EDITS: Book 2 Ch 2

Use colour edits to:

- fix colour erros the camera makes
- enhance the colour in an image
- change the colours completely, including converting to B&W

NOTES

Date:

HOMEWORK

- ☐ over-saturate an image

- ☐ compare saturation and vibrance

- ☐ create 3 different black and white edits on the same original image

- ☐ use colour temperature to radically change the feel of an image

- ☐ change a blue sky using selective colour adjustments

- ☐ change the saturation of just a single colour

TO DO

Do you know the difference between RAW and JPEG? Which will you shoot, and why?

REVISION

- ☐ use composition to create a static image

Monday

Tuesday

Wednesday

Thursday

Friday

Saturday

Sunday

WEEK 25: Edit 3

TONAL EDITS: Book 2 Ch 3

Learn to tell the difference between the shadows, midtones and highlights of an image. Be aware of whether you have any true blacks or true whites.

Once you can edit individual tones separately you will have a much finer control over your whole image.

NOTES

Date:

HOMEWORK

☐ compare changing
contrast and clarity

☐ see what effect an
S-curve has on 3 tonally
very different images

☐ try extreme tonal edits
using only the tone curve

TO DO

Try a Lightroom 30 day
free trial. Watch these 7
short videos to get started
quickly:

emmadaviesphotography.
com/blog/getting-started-
with-lightroom

REVISION

☐ use the rule of thirds

Monday

Tuesday

Wednesday

Thursday

Friday

Saturday

Sunday

WEEK 26: Edit 4

ADVANCED EDITS: Book 2 Ch 4

Advanced edits include
- using graduated filters
- using adjustment brushes
- split toning
- sharpening
- cloning

NOTES

Date:

HOMEWORK

- ☐ use a rectangular graduated filter to bring back sky detail

- ☐ use a radial graduated filter to brighten your focal point

- ☐ use an adjustment brush to "paint" brightness onto your image

- ☐ split tone a black and white image

- ☐ split tone a coloured image

- ☐ try cloning or spot removal

TO DO

Research sharpening, and find out how to do it with your preferred software.

REVISION

- ☐ fill the frame with your subject

Monday

Tuesday

Wednesday

Thursday

Friday

Saturday

Sunday

WEEK 27: Have a break

NOTES from Edit module

What are your views on editing images?

Date:

	Monday
	Tuesday
	Wednesday
	Thursday
	Friday
	Saturday
	Sunday

END OF EDIT MODULE - CONSOLIDATE

- [ ] brighten a photo using local edits only
- [ ] crop 3 ways for 3 different compositions
- [ ] make 3 different images have the same white balance
- [ ] increase vibrance of whole image and then selectively reduce the saturation of just 1 colour
- [ ] create a low contrast black and white image
- [ ] use a radial graduated filter to make a vignette
- [ ] use a rectangular graduated filter to change the sky
- [ ] change the tone curve and see what happens to the histogram

END OF EDIT MODULE - PROJECT

Doing the last 20%

- [ ] fix exposure errors
- [ ] consider tonal adjustments
- [ ] consider local colour adjustments
- [ ] try a different crop
- [ ] walk away for at least an hour
- [ ] zoom to 100% and look for dust spots
- [ ] take a copy and size as needed
- [ ] sharpen based on end use

The glory is not in never falling, but in rising every time we fall.

~ attributed to Oliver Goldsmith

WEEK 28: Tripod 1

MOTION BLUR: Book 2 Ch 5

By locking your camera down on a tripod to avoid camera shake, and then using a long shutter speed, you can deliberately create the effect where anything in the image that moves (like water, or clouds) will record as a blur whilst the rest of the image will stay sharp.

NOTES

Date:

HOMEWORK

☐ use a long shutter speed
to catch motion blur

TO DO

If you don't have a tripod, try
a pile of books + self timer.

REVISION

☐ shoot a contrejour image

Monday	
Tuesday	
Wednesday	
Thursday	
Friday	
Saturday	
Sunday	

WEEK 29: Tripod 2

MAXIMUM DEPTH OF FIELD: Book 2 Ch 6

When you want a large depth of field (and therefore will be using a small aperture), you need to watch your shutter speed carefully. Once it creeps over the maximum you can safely hand hold, you will need to use a tripod.

NOTES

Date:

HOMEWORK

☐ maximise your depth
of field using a small
aperture, a tripod, a low
ISO and the self timer

TO DO

Work out how to use your
self timer, and use it to
minimise camera shake with
longer shutter speeds.

REVISION

☐ shoot the same subject
with both hard and soft
shadows

Monday

Tuesday

Wednesday

Thursday

Friday

Saturday

Sunday

WEEK 30: Tripod 3

MULTIPLE EXPOSURES: Book 2 Ch 7

If you can guarantee that the camera will not move between shots (by using a tripod), you can try more creative photography including this week's project - time lapse photography.

NOTES

Date:

HOMEWORK

☐ shoot a timelapse of at least 3 images

REVISION

☐ have 2 colours of light in the same image

TO DO

Learn how to turn your timelapse images into a GIF.

Monday

Tuesday

Wednesday

Thursday

Friday

Saturday

Sunday

WEEK 31: Tripod 4

HANDS FREE: Book 2 Ch 8

A tripod is not essential for this week's project - it is just a lot easier to be able to set your camera down safely in one place and have an extra pair of hands to deal with your subject matter.

NOTES

Date:

HOMEWORK

☐ try water splash photography safely - do not risk getting water on your electronics.

REVISION

☐ use the wrong colour temperature for your conditions

TO DO

Learn how to bracket your shots.

Monday

Tuesday

Wednesday

Thursday

Friday

Saturday

Sunday

WEEK 32: Have a break

Notes from Tripod module

Can you see the benefits of being able to stablise your camera before you press the shutter?

Date:

	Monday
	Tuesday
	Wednesday
	Thursday
	Friday
	Saturday
	Sunday

END OF TRIPOD MODULE - REVISION

- [ ] subject in focus, background blurred
- [ ] large depth of field
- [ ] shot at f16
- [ ] creative camera shake
- [ ] shot at 1/500th
- [ ] shot on ISO 1600
- [ ] shot at your closest focussing distance
- [ ] moving subject frozen
- [ ] 2 second exposure
- [ ] remember: subject, foreground, background
- [ ] use symmetry
- [ ] use a mirror as a reflector to create a fill light
- [ ] shoot a photograph with no shadows
- [ ] turn an image black and white in editing
- [ ] crop an image to make it more dramatic

END OF TRIPOD MODULE - PROJECT

You are approximately half way through the year. Besides completing the revision topics above, you can take this opportunity to go back and finish one of the tripod homework topics. Do the extra 20% - plan it, execute it, edit it, print it.

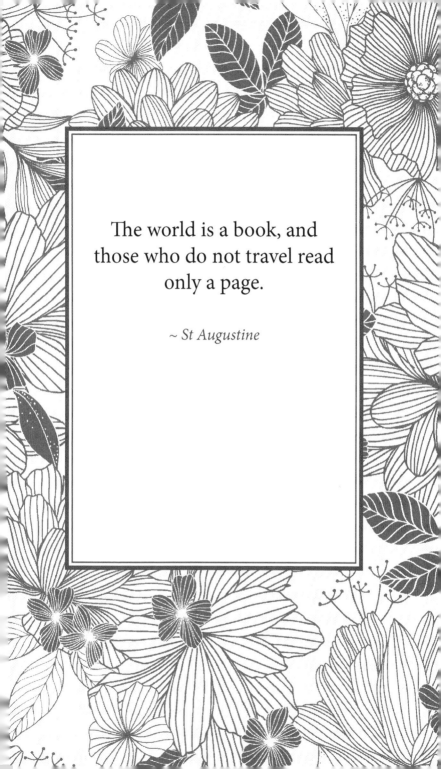

The world is a book, and
those who do not travel read
only a page.

~ St Augustine

WEEK 33: Travel/Composition 1

RESEARCH: Book 2 Ch 14

If you have Book 2, this section corresponds to the Travel module. If you do not, take the next 4 weeks as a break. You can either go back over something you want to revisit, or take part in 30 Days Of Composition.

For 30 Days of Composition, shoot an image every day for a month, using the suggested daily prompt.

NOTES

Share your composition images on Instagram with the hashtag #30DaysOfComposition.

Date:

HOMEWORK

- [ ] visit a new destination and take unplanned photographs

30 DAYS OF COMPOSITION

- [ ] viewpoint
- [ ] framing
- [ ] negative space
- [ ] diagonals
- [ ] rule of thirds
- [ ] leading lines
- [ ] symmetry

Monday

Tuesday

Wednesday

Thursday

Friday

Saturday

Sunday

WEEK 34: Travel/Composition 2

DOCUMENTING A HOLIDAY: Book 2 Ch 15

Cultivate a mindset of compromise whilst on holiday: compromise over kit, and compromise over time dedicated to photography. Use your phone when you need to.

Develop the skill of visual storytelling.

NOTES

Date:

HOMEWORK

- ☐ using only your phone, or camera on auto, tell the story of a day or weekend in your life

30 DAYS OF COMPOSITION

- ☐ fill the frame
- ☐ threes or fives
- ☐ balance
- ☐ pattern
- ☐ no foreground
- ☐ circular
- ☐ form or shape

Monday

Tuesday

Wednesday

Thursday

Friday

Saturday

Sunday

WEEK 35: Travel/Composition 3

TRAVELLING LOCALLY: Book 2 Ch 16

Don't overlook local places. You can use days out to rehearse for bigger trips - to make sure your kit works, you have enough spare batteries, and you have an idea of how to capture the whole place not just the views.

NOTES

Date:

HOMEWORK

- [ ] visit a new place and spend at least a day there taking photographs

30 DAYS OF COMPOSITION

- [ ] texture
- [ ] what's leaving the frame?
- [ ] create depth
- [ ] create movement
- [ ] perfectly aligned
- [ ] deliberately discordant
- [ ] square format

Monday

Tuesday

Wednesday

Thursday

Friday

Saturday

Sunday

WEEK 36: Travel/Composition 4

DESTINATION PHOTOGRAPHY: Book 2 Ch 17

Travel responsibly. Think about the impact your visit will have.

Do your research, know your kit, be able to tell a story.

Plan your logistics, and have a trial run to test your kit.

NOTES

Date:

HOMEWORK

☐ make a list of objections and solutions to the question of what is stopping you taking a trip dedicated to photography

30 DAYS OF COMPOSITION

☐ single focal point
☐ tiny subject
☐ complementary colour
☐ mono
☐ abstract
☐ repetition
☐ S-curve
☐ eye contact
☐ break the rules

Monday

Tuesday

Wednesday

Thursday

Friday

Saturday

Sunday

WEEK 37: Have a break

**Notes from Travel module and/or
30 Days of Composition**

You are more than half way through the course. Think back to day 1. What has changed about your mindset when it comes to photography, and what technical skills do you possess now that you didn't before?

Date:

	Monday
	Tuesday
	Wednesday
	Thursday
	Friday
	Saturday
	Sunday

END OF TRAVEL MODULE - REVISION

- ☐ shoot a silhouette
- ☐ shoot a sunset, exposed how you want it to be
- ☐ take a photo of wildlife: one frozen and one blurred
- ☐ 3 shots of a building with the light coming from 3 directions
- ☐ 5 images that tell the story of a journey
- ☐ 3 images with different apertures - changed without looking
- ☐ blur moving people out of a scene with a long shutter speed
- ☐ a phone photo so good you can't tell it was taken on a phone
- ☐ an environmental portait
- ☐ white on white, with the exposure right first time
- ☐ an abstract shot using a long shutter speed

END OF TRAVEL MODULE - PROJECT

Create a photobook of a holiday, or finish 3 prints from a photo trip and get them on the wall.

If you just did 30 Days Of Composition, pick your 3 favourites, edit them, and print them.

The important thing is to actually do the homework, not just say you will do it. For the travel project you don't have to go on a new trip - you can create something from a visit you've already been on.

Remember your story arc. Set the scene, introduce characters, add tension, create a resolution.

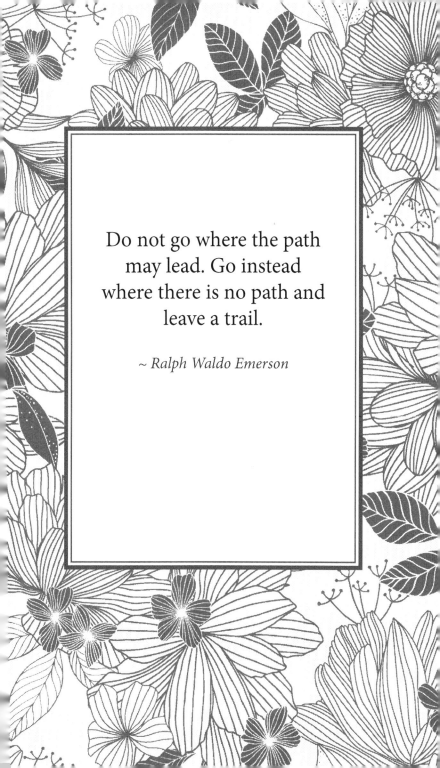

Do not go where the path
may lead. Go instead
where there is no path and
leave a trail.

~ *Ralph Waldo Emerson*

WEEK 38: Landscape 1

LIGHT FOR LANDSCAPE: Book 2 Ch 9/10

The direction, colour and quality of light are what lifts a
landscape image from a snapshot to a work of art. There is no
right or wrong light, but you do need to look closely and see
how the light is reacting with the land before you press the
shutter.

NOTES

Date:

HOMEWORK

☐ start a collection of images of the same view in as many different weather conditions as possible, and at as many times throughout the day and year as you can manage.

TO DO

1. Research 5 landscape photographers you had not previously heard of. What do they have in common, and what makes them different?

2. Go through the planner and mark in some regular reminders to build up your homework collection at different times of the year.

REVISION

☐ take a shot on auto mode, then take the same shot on manual mode but change all 3 settings whilst keeping the exposure the same

Monday

Tuesday

Wednesday

Thursday

Friday

Saturday

Sunday

WEEK 39: Landscape 2

EXPOSURE FOR LANDSCAPE: Book 2 Ch 11

After finding the light, your next challenge is dealing with the fact that the dynamic range of your camera's sensor is much smaller than that of your eye. You will see detail in shadows and highlights that your camera cannot resolve in the image so you either need to pick which one will be correctly exposed, or use the techniques described in Chapter 11 of Book 2 to extend the dynamic range of your camera.

NOTES

Date:

HOMEWORK

☐ take a photograph where the sky is correctly exposed - ignore what is happening to the foreground

REVISION

☐ Do you remember the 3 metering modes, and how each one works? Can you activate each of them?

☐ Can you remember how to read the histogram, to see what the camera is seeing? And how to use exposure compensation mode (or manual mode) to adjust the exposure?

Monday

Tuesday

Wednesday

Thursday

Friday

Saturday

Sunday

WEEK 40: Landscape 3

SETTINGS FOR LANDSCAPE: Book 2 Ch 12

To be a landscape photographer you cannot hide behind small mistakes, or not quite understand what the camera is doing. You need to take control of aperture, shutter speed and ISO, often in the wind and the rain.

NOTES

Date:

HOMEWORK

- ☐ f22 long focus
- ☐ f22 hyperfocal distance
- ☐ f8 long focus
- ☐ f8 hyperfocal distance

REVISION

- ☐ Can you change aperture, shutter speed and ISO without looking?

Monday

Tuesday

Wednesday

Thursday

Friday

Saturday

Sunday

WEEK 41: Landscape 4

COMPOSITION FOR LANDSCAPE:
Book 2 Ch 13

The final piece in the puzzle for compelling landscape photographs is the composition. Every single thing in the frame must earn its place. Don't forget that the thing that will control your composition is your feet: where you stand affects where everything appears in the frame.

NOTES

Date:

HOMEWORK

Practise epic composition.

- ☐ where will you stand?
- ☐ where does the eye go first?
- ☐ where does the eye go next?
- ☐ is that where you want it to go?
- ☐ is anything overlapping, and if so is that what you want?
- ☐ are there any black holes?
- ☐ how is your background/ subject/foreground balance?
- ☐ what's going on at the edge of the frame?
- ☐ what distractions are there and can you get rid of them?
- ☐ what happens if you move?

Monday

Tuesday

Wednesday

Thursday

Friday

Saturday

Sunday

WEEK 42: Have a break

Notes from Landscape module

Landscape photography is the most challenging and most rewarding of all the disciplines. How did you get on? What do you want to work on?

Date:

	Monday
	Tuesday
	Wednesday
	Thursday
	Friday
	Saturday
	Sunday

END OF LANDSCAPE MODULE - REVISION

- [ ] shot in the style of Michael Kenna
- [ ] shot in the style of an Outdoor Photo magazine cover
- [ ] lit from the front/back/sides, shot at the same time of day
- [ ] landscape with very strong side lighting
- [ ] landscape with very flat light
- [ ] shot before, during and after dawn or sunset
- [ ] use the wrong colour temp settings for your conditions
- [ ] get 2 colours of light in the same landscape
- [ ] use nothing but spot metering for a week
- [ ] use hyperfocal distance to maximise depth of field
- [ ] an image with a circular path for the eye to follow
- [ ] an image with an S-shape for the eye to follow
- [ ] an image where the eye is encouraged to leave the frame

END OF LANDSCAPE MODULE - PROJECT

Take a landscape image you are proud of, and get it on your wall.

- [ ] pick a style and a destination
- [ ] research locations, viewpoints, weather
- [ ] arrive early and let the landscape speak to you
- [ ] prepare your composition and settings
- [ ] wait for the light if you need to
- [ ] review and revise as needed

Blessed are they who see
beautiful things in humble
places where other people
see nothing.

~ *Pissarro*

WEEK 43: Macro 1

YOUR 1ST MACRO SHOT: Book 2 Ch 18

You cannot skip the fundamentals or cut corners with close up photography. All your small mistakes will be magnified along with everything else.

Can you remember everything you've learnt about aperture, shutter speed, metering and focus?

NOTES

Date:

HOMEWORK

10 steps for macro success:

- ☐ tripod
- ☐ indirect light
- ☐ aperture priority mode
- ☐ low ISO
- ☐ stable subject
- ☐ mirror lock up
- ☐ minimum focussing distance
- ☐ manual focus
- ☐ how does it look?
- ☐ self timer

Monday

Tuesday

Wednesday

Thursday

Friday

Saturday

Sunday

WEEK 44: Macro 2

DEPTH OF FIELD: Book 2 Ch 19

The main thing to remember is that you will be working with a depth of field that is only millimetres deep in some cases. Pay particular attention to out of focus areas that can lose all detail and become unattractive.

NOTES

Date:

HOMEWORK

Repeat last week's homework, but pay careful attention to the relationship between focussing distance, aperture and depth of field.

- ☐ minimum focussing distance and all the available full stop apertures

- ☐ move slightly further away and repeat: and all the available full stop apertures

Monday

Tuesday

Wednesday

Thursday

Friday

Saturday

Sunday

WEEK 45: Macro 3

EXPOSURE: Book 2 Ch 20

You need to be very precise with your metering to get an accurate exposure first time with macro photography. Either work with spot metering and pick something approximately 18% grey to meter from, or be prepared to make adjustments as you go in manual mode or with the exposure compensation dial.

NOTES

Date:

HOMEWORK

- ☐ work out how to use spot metering, and how to change the focus points

- ☐ practise spot metering off something that is approximately 18% grey

- ☐ try using a grey card to fix your exposure before you start a macro session

- ☐ try using spot metering for macro - how easy is it to find the right spot to meter from?

Monday
Tuesday
Wednesday
Thursday
Friday
Saturday
Sunday

WEEK 46: Macro 4

LIGHT AND COMPOSITION: Book 2 Ch 21

The quality and direction of light plays a big part in macro photography because, along with everything else, it is magnified. Harsh shadows take over an image, and bright highlights become distracting.

Pay close attention to the light, and include it as a separate element as you build your composition.

NOTES

Date:

HOMEWORK

☐ Take a series of macro images of the same subject in different lights and from different angles.

Review all the images critically, and look out for anything unexpected that has appeared.

Monday	
Tuesday	
Wednesday	
Thursday	
Friday	
Saturday	
Sunday	

WEEK 47: Have a break

Notes from Macro module

There's nowhere to hide with macro photography. Did you find this module has helped your overall technical confidence?

Date:

	Monday
	Tuesday
	Wednesday
	Thursday
	Friday
	Saturday
	Sunday

END OF MACRO MODULE - TEST

Consolidate your knowledge by taking these macro photos:

- [ ] fill the frame
- [ ] include some background
- [ ] an insect
- [ ] a coin with front to back depth of field
- [ ] shallow depth of field to obscure the identity of the subject
- [ ] a table top, or something with texture
- [ ] hand held, but no camera shake
- [ ] very soft shadows
- [ ] shot in direct light but still looks good
- [ ] use a grey card to get the exposure right first time
- [ ] shot on manual mode

END OF MACRO MODULE - PROJECT

Work on a portfolio of 6 macro images that sit together as a group.

A portfolio needs to be consistent, so pick either the same or similar subject, or choose a series with a theme.

Once you have all 6 images finished, print them and hang them on a wall.

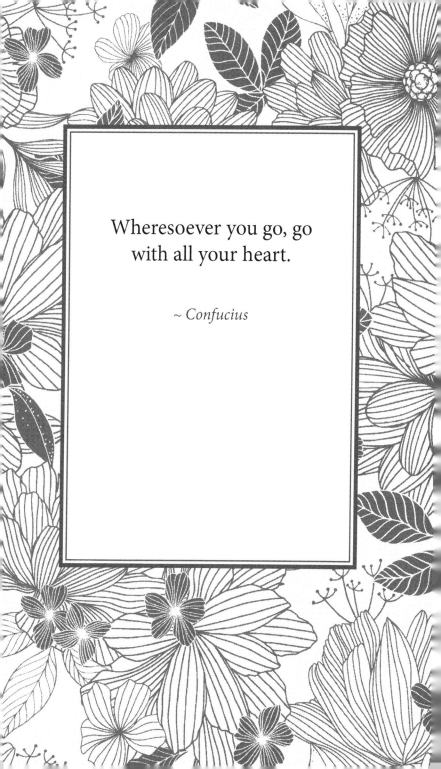

Wheresoever you go, go
with all your heart.

~ *Confucius*

WEEK 48: Share 1

WORKFLOW: Book 2 Ch 22

Your future self will thank you for starting to organise your digital photography workflow this week. The aims are simply to make it easier to find images, and to protect your photos from loss.

NOTES

Date:

HOMEWORK

Just start with the next thing today, and keep adding steps throughout the month.

- [ ] download & keyword
- [ ] backup
- [ ] import admin
- [ ] edit & backup
- [ ] share & sharpen
- [ ] archive

Monday
Tuesday
Wednesday
Thursday
Friday
Saturday
Sunday

WEEK 49: Share 2

PRINTS: Book 2 Ch 23

When it comes to sharing prints, done is always better than perfect. Work out what's stopping you from getting your images in print form, and address that head on.

Start giving prints away to friends and family again.

NOTES

Date:

HOMEWORK

☐ get 12 images up on your wall in a temporary display; or

☐ start work on getting one of your best images printed big, framed, and on the wall

Monday

Tuesday

Wednesday

Thursday

Friday

Saturday

Sunday

WEEK 50: Share 3

ONLINE SHARING: Book 2 Ch 24

You need to strike your own balance between convenience and privacy when it comes to online sharing. Don't rule it out all together - there are plenty of ways to share without telling the whole world about it.

NOTES

Date:

HOMEWORK

☐ have you ever shared images online?

☐ start sharing again - think of a couple of people who would love to get a photo from you, even if just by email

☐ what's stopping you joining a social sharing platform like Instagram or Blipfoto?

☐ are you attracted by the idea of meeting other photographers online?

☐ do you know how to find the privacy controls for any online sharing platforms you use?

☐ what can you do to build online sharing into your digital workflow?

Monday

Tuesday

Wednesday

Thursday

Friday

Saturday

Sunday

WEEK 51: Share 4

PRINTED BOOKS: Book 2 Ch 25

Holding a printed book full of your images is the most satisfying feeling for any photographer. It's the end of the year. Celebrate making it this far by designing and printing a book to commemorate your journey.

NOTES

Date:

HOMEWORK

- [ ] create a photo book or a photo album

Monday

Tuesday

Wednesday

Thursday

Friday

Saturday

Sunday

WEEK 52: End of Year

Looking back and looking forwards

List the 3 things you are most proud of achieving:

What did you find challenging this year, and what did you do about it?

What do you want to conquer next year? List at least 3:

Who can you share your photographs with? List 3 people you will send prints to:

Date:

	Monday
	Tuesday
	Wednesday
	Thursday
	Friday
	Saturday
	Sunday

Notes

67348500R00077

4Made in the USA
Lexington, KY
09 September 2017